Today's
Superst★rs
Entertainment

Oprah Winfrey

By Jayne Keedle

Gareth Stevens
Publishing

Please visit our web site at www.garethstevens.com.
For a free color catalog describing our list of high-quality books,
call 1-800-542-2595 (USA) or 1-800-387-3178 (Canada). Our fax: 1-877-542-2596

Library of Congress Cataloging-in-Publication Data
Keedle, Jayne.
  Oprah Winfrey / by Jayne Keedle.
      p. cm. — (Today's superstars : entertainment)
  Includes bibliographical references and index.
  ISBN-13: 978-0-8368-9238-3 (lib. bdg. : alk. paper)
  ISBN-10: 0-8368-9238-0 (lib. bdg. : alk. paper)
  1. Winfrey, Oprah—Juvenile literature. 2. Television personalities—
  United States—Biography—Juvenile literature. 3. Actors—United States—
  Biography—Juvenile literature. I. Title.
  PN1992.4.W56K44   2009
  791.4502'8092—dc22 [B]   2008013917

This edition first published in 2009 by
Gareth Stevens Publishing
A Weekly Reader® Company
1 Reader's Digest Road
Pleasantville, NY 10570-7000 USA

Senior Managing Editor: Lisa M. Herrington
Senior Editor: Brian Fitzgerald
Creative Director: Lisa Donovan
Senior Designer: Keith Plechaty
Production Designer: Cynthia Malaran
Photo Researcher: Kim Babbitt

Photo credits: cover Bill Davila/FilmMagic/Getty Images; title page, p. 25
King World Productions/courtesy Everett Collection; p. 5 Michelly Rall/Getty
Images; p. 7 AFP/Getty Images; p. 9 courtesy of the Star-Herald; p. 11 Nashville
Historical Society; p. 13 Film Magic/Getty Images; p. 15 Warner Brothers/
courtesy Everett Collection; p. 17 Everett Collection; p. 18 Cynthia Johnson/
Getty Images; p. 19 Reuters/Corbis; p. 20 SGranitz/Getty Images; p. 21 AFP/
Getty Images; p. 23 AP Images; p. 27 Wire Images/Getty Images; p. 28
Per-Anders Petterson/Getty Images.

Printed in the United States

1 2 3 4 5 6 7 8 9 10 09 08

Contents

Words in the glossary appear in **bold** type the first time they are used in the text.

Chapter 1

Viva Oprah!

Word of Oprah Winfrey's arrival spread quickly through Soweto. Even in the poor South African town, everyone knows Oprah. A growing crowd chanted, "Viva, Oprah Winfrey, Viva!"

The TV host's visit was a surprise. She had another surprise for two Soweto girls. Standing in their family's two-room shack, Oprah delivered the good news.

The girls would be among the first 150 students at the Oprah Winfrey Leadership Academy for Girls. The girls screamed in delight. Onlookers were moved to tears of joy. Oprah, as always, was ready with a hug for her school's two newest students.

Smiling students joined Oprah at the opening of her school in South Africa.

Not Just All Talk

As host of *The Oprah Winfrey Show,* she reaches millions of people every day. Yet Oprah is much more than a talk show host. She runs her own company, publishes magazines, manages charities—and builds schools, too. Hard work has brought her wealth and power. Oprah uses both to help other people.

Fact File

Oprah used to dream of the girls who would go to her school. In her dream, their faces were blurry. She would ask, "What is your name?" She would wake up before they could tell her. Now Oprah knows their names by heart.

A Dream Come True

"The greatest gift I know you can give is the gift of learning," says Oprah. "I believe that my own success has come from a love of learning." Like the girls she chose to attend her academy, Oprah grew up poor. "I had nothing as a girl. Education was my path to possibility."

The Oprah Winfrey Leadership Academy opened on January 2, 2007. Reporters and Hollywood stars flew to South Africa for the event. With her students by her side, Oprah cut a red ribbon and opened the $40 million academy. "This is a school for powerful girls who will use their power in service to their nation and to our world," Oprah said.

Fact File

Time magazine named Oprah one of the 100 Most Influential People in the World each year from 2004 to 2008.

6

Nelson Mandela and
Oprah shared a laugh
in December 2002.

A Promise to Keep

From 1948 to 1989, a policy called **apartheid** divided South Africa by
race. Black South Africans were poor and had no political power. The
law limited where they could live, work, and go to school.

Nelson Mandela fought to end apartheid. His battle landed him in
prison for 27 years. Yet he never gave up. His release from prison in
1989 signaled the end of apartheid. In 1994, South Africans of all races
voted for the first time. They chose Mandela as president. The South
African people fondly call him Madiba, a title given to tribal elders.

In 2000, Oprah met Mandela. She asked him what gift she might give
the South African people. Mandela asked her to build a school. "I made
a promise to Madiba," Oprah said, "and I intend to keep it."

Chapter 2

A Rocky Beginning

Oprah's path to success was rocky at first. She was born on January 29, 1954, in the small town of Kosciusko, Mississippi. Her mother, Vernita Lee, was 18 when Oprah was born. Her father, Vernon Winfrey, was a young soldier at a nearby military base. Her parents never married. Vernon didn't know about Oprah until Vernita wrote to him to ask him to send clothes. By then, Vernon was stationed far away.

In the 1950s, many African Americans left the South to find work. Oprah's mother was one of them. Vernita moved north to Milwaukee, Wisconsin. She took a job as a maid. She left Oprah behind in Mississippi.

Fact File

Oprah has an unusual name. Her great-aunt wanted to name her Orpah, after a woman in the Bible's Book of Ruth. The name was misspelled on her birth certificate.

Coming Home

Oprah lived with **racism** as a child. **Jim Crow laws** in the South kept African Americans separate from white people. African Americans were unable to get good jobs or a good education.

In 2006, Oprah returned to Kosciusko, Mississippi, to open a Boys & Girls Club. She donated $6.5 million to the center. "There was no place like that in Mississippi when I was growing up," she wrote in *O, The Oprah Magazine*. "Even if there had been, Jim Crow laws would have locked me out. Now everyone is welcome."

Oprah gave a speech at the opening of the Boys & Girls Club in her hometown.

Life With Hattie Mae

Until Oprah was 6, she was raised by her grandmother Hattie Mae. They lived on a small farm. They had no electricity or running water. Hattie Mae believed in old-fashioned discipline. If Oprah misbehaved, her grandmother would whip her. Still, Hattie Mae encouraged Oprah to learn. "I am what I am because of my grandmother," Oprah says. By age 3, Oprah could read. She learned to write before she entered kindergarten.

Fact File

On her first day of kindergarten, Oprah wrote a note to her teacher. It read, "Dear Miss New: I do not think I belong here." Her teacher agreed. Oprah skipped ahead to first grade.

It's a Hard Knock Life

When Oprah turned 6, life changed. She moved to Milwaukee to join her mother. Vernita worked hard to support them. She had little time for Oprah. She had even less time after Oprah's half-sister Patricia was born. A third child, Oprah's half-brother Jeffrey, was born a few years later.

Vernita often left Oprah in the care of people who were not trustworthy. At age 9, Oprah was abused by an older cousin. Another relative and a friend of her mother's also abused her. Oprah told no one. She didn't feel that she had anyone to turn to for help.

A Troubled Teen

Oprah kept her pain private but turned her anger outward. She began getting into trouble. She often stayed out late and lied about what she was doing. At 13, Oprah ran away from home. Vernita was unable to cope with her wild child. She sent Oprah to Nashville, Tennessee, to live with her father and stepmother instead.

Fact File

Oprah was always an excellent public speaker. She was often paid to speak at churches. After one speech, she told her father that she had found her calling. She wanted to be paid to talk for a living!

Life With Father

Vernon Winfrey and his wife Zelma were determined to get Oprah back on track. Her father had strict rules and tight curfews. He expected Oprah to get good grades in school. Zelma insisted that Oprah read a book a week and write a report on it. Oprah blossomed.

During her senior year of high school, Oprah's class visited a local radio station. An employee noticed Oprah's gift for speaking on air. The station gave her a job reading the news. In 1971, she enrolled at Tennessee State University to study speech communication and theater.

Oprah was named Nashville's Miss Fire Prevention in 1971. She was also crowned Miss Black Tennessee.

Chapter 3
Making News

Oprah was still in college when she got her first job in television. In 1973, she became a reporter at WTVF-TV in Nashville. At 19, she was the youngest person, and the first African American, to co-anchor news at the station. Later, Oprah moved to Baltimore, Maryland, to take a job as co-anchor of the evening news at WJZ-TV.

As a reporter, Oprah was supposed to read the news without emotion. Yet she couldn't help but react to the stories. She laughed at funny stories and cried at sad ones. In 1978, Oprah took a new job at the station. She became cohost of a talk show called *People Are Talking*. At that moment, Oprah says, "I knew that I was home. I felt like I could be myself."

Talk About Success!

In 1983, Oprah moved again, this time to Chicago, Illinois. At the start of 1984, she became host of WLS-TV's morning talk show, *A.M. Chicago*. Oprah's new show faced some tough competition. It aired at the same time as the top-rated *Phil Donahue Show*. Yet after just one month, Oprah's was the number-one talk show in Chicago. Local headlines proclaimed, "Oprah Dwarfs Donahue!"

Gayle King and Oprah have been best friends for almost 30 years.

Best Friends

Oprah met her best friend, Gayle King, when the two worked at WJZ-TV in Baltimore. Their friendship began during a snowstorm. Gayle couldn't make it home from work, so Oprah invited her to stay over. The two stayed up all night talking, like teens at a sleepover. They have talked almost every day since then.

Gayle is editor-at-large of *O, The Oprah Magazine*. She is also active with Oprah's charities. Oprah trusts Gayle to always be honest with her. "There is a level of mutual respect that comes from being with somebody you know doesn't want anything from you but you," Oprah said in an interview for *O, The Oprah Magazine*.

Harpo Studios

Only three women have run their own entertainment studios. The first was silent-movie star Mary Pickford. She helped start United Artists in 1919. Comedy legend Lucille Ball helped found Desilu Studios in the 1950s. With Harpo, Oprah joined this special group.

Since 1990, *The Oprah Winfrey Show* has been taped at Harpo Studios in Chicago. The company grew to become Harpo, Inc., a **multimedia** empire with more than 400 employees. Oprah jokes that she built her own studio so she could bring her dogs to work!

Taking Control

Oprah's personality and charm made the show a success. The show's **producers** knew it. In 1985, they renamed it *The Oprah Winfrey Show*. Life was good, but Oprah wanted more control over her show. In 1986, she formed her own company, Harpo, Inc. That same year, the show began to air nationwide. For the first time, viewers across the country would see *The Oprah Winfrey Show.*

The night before her national **debut**, Oprah wrote in her journal. "I keep wondering how my life will change, if it will change, and what this all means," she wrote. She didn't know that her life was about to change in a big way!

Fact File

How did Oprah come up with the name of her company? *Harpo* is *Oprah* spelled backward!

The Color Purple

Oprah believes in working hard to achieve her dreams. She also believes that some things are in God's hands. She says that winning the role of Sofia in the 1985 film *The Color Purple* was one of those things.

The Color Purple, by Alice Walker, is one of Oprah's favorite books. She used to carry spare copies of the book to give away to friends who hadn't read it. "I have never wanted anything in my life, before or since, as much as I wanted to be in *The Color Purple*," she said.

Oprah **auditioned** but was told she didn't have much of a chance. She prayed for grace in defeat. Oprah was mid-prayer when she learned that she had won the part. She earned an Oscar nomination for her performance. The Oscars are the top awards for movies.

Chapter 4

Every Person Matters

As a talk show host, Oprah was an instant hit with viewers. Part of her appeal is that she meets everyone as a friend. She invites famous people to hang out at pajama parties and gives poor people star treatment. Oprah says that years of interviewing people taught her one big lesson: "Every person matters."

Oprah is a good and **sympathetic** listener. Her honesty and openness inspire people to talk about tough topics. She often focuses on the concerns of ordinary people. In the early 1990s, many talk shows turned trashy. They covered subjects that were in poor taste. To get ratings, some hosts even encouraged guests to get into fistfights. Oprah wanted no part of that trend.

One of Oprah's best qualities is being a good listener.

Higher Standards

In 1994, Oprah said her show would focus only on "uplifting, meaningful subjects." Audiences and **critics** approved of her approach. *The Oprah Winfrey Show* continued to earn strong ratings and win awards. That year, Oprah earned her fifth Emmy Award for best talk show host. The Emmys are the top awards for TV shows.

People open up to Oprah because she is equally open about her own life. "Just tell the truth," she says. "It'll save you every time." On her show, Oprah talked about the abuse she suffered as a child.

Protecting Children

Oprah wanted to protect children from the same abuses she suffered. In 1991, she asked Congress to pass the National Child Protection Act. In 1993, the "Oprah Bill" become law. It created a national **database** of child abusers.

The Oprah Effect

When Oprah does something, people take notice. In 1996, she started Oprah's Book Club. Suddenly, millions of people were buying the books she recommended. Every book picked for the club has become a best seller. Publishers call it "the Oprah effect."

Fact File

In 1999, the National Book Foundation awarded Oprah its 50th Anniversary Gold Medal for service to books and authors.

Hooked on Books

Oprah didn't create the book club to sell books. She did it because she loves to read. "When I didn't have friends," she says, "I had books." Oprah picks each book for the club. Whenever possible, she invites the authors to her show to talk about their work. "Authors are like gods to me," she says.

Oprah's Book Club has launched the careers of up-and-coming authors. She has also introduced people to classic literature. Oprah's Book Club put John Steinbeck's novel *East of Eden* back on the best-seller list some 40 years after the author's death.

Author Toni Morrison (left) is one of Oprah's heroes. Morrison's book *Song of Solomon* was a book club pick in 1996.

Oprah has taken part in many walks and runs for charity.

Battling the Bulge

Oprah is always honest with her viewers. She has been open about her struggles with her weight. Over the years, Oprah has lost 90 pounds and gained as much as 65. She knew that other people were fighting the same battle. If she found a diet-and-exercise plan that worked, she shared it with viewers. When diets failed, she was honest about her feelings, too.

In 1994, Oprah celebrated her 40th birthday in a special way. She ran a marathon in Washington, D.C. In 1996, she co-authored a book with health-and-fitness expert Bob Greene. She hopes to help other people win the fight to be fit. "Getting my lifelong weight struggle under control has come from a process of treating myself as well as I treat others in every way," Oprah wrote in *O, The Oprah Magazine*.

Spreading the Word

Oprah has shown she can sell magazines, too. In 2000, she started *O, The Oprah Magazine.* It was one of the most successful magazine launches in history. Like Oprah's show, the magazine aims to help people live healthier and more spiritual lives. *The Oprah Magazine* now has about 16 million readers. A South African version of the magazine launched in 2002. Two years later, Oprah created a second magazine, *O at Home.*

Fact File

Oprah took *The Oprah Winfrey Show* out of the running for future Emmy Awards in 2000. At that time, the show had won more than 40 Emmys. Oprah received a Lifetime Achievement Award in 1998.

Chapter 5 Making a Difference

"When you learn, teach. When you get, give." Oprah says that her friend poet Maya Angelou taught her that. Oprah tries to live by those words. In 1987, she created the Oprah Winfrey Foundation to help women and children in need. The foundation has given millions of dollars to charities around the world.

In December 2002, Oprah visited orphanages in South Africa. She delivered food, clothing, school supplies, and toys to 50,000 children. Sixty-three schools also received libraries and teacher training. During that trip, Oprah broke ground with Nelson Mandela on the school she had promised to build.

Fact File

Oprah is a believer in a strong education. The Oprah Winfrey Scholars Program pays tuition for U.S. students who plan to use their education to help others.

Angels in Our Midst

Oprah encourages other people to help, too. In 1998, she founded Oprah's Angel Network. She got the idea from a young girl named Nora. Nora and her friends collected pennies. They raised $400,000 for charity.

Oprah asked viewers to join her Angel Network and donate loose change. The goal was to fund 50 student scholarships. Within 10 months, the network had raised nearly $3.7 million. That was enough for pay tuition for one student from every state for three years. "That is how small change makes a difference," Oprah said.

Oprah helped thousands of children during her 2002 trip to South Africa.

23

Katrina Homes

Oprah's Angels flew into action when Hurricane Katrina struck in 2005. After traveling to the devastated Gulf Coast states with supplies of food and water, Oprah asked viewers to get involved. They responded by donating more than $15 million. In addition, Oprah personally pledged $10 million. All told, Oprah's Angel Network has built or restored nearly 300 homes in four states.

Making Dreams Come True

For years, Oprah has used her show to make people's dreams come true. She has given away scholarships, homes, money, and cars. In 2008, she went a step further. *Oprah's Big Give*, a prime-time series on ABC, gave away millions of dollars to people in need.

Oprah Winfrey Presents ...

In high school, Oprah dreamed of being an actor. Now she's also interested in producing films. Harpo Films creates made-for-TV movies under the heading "Oprah Winfrey Presents." Many of them are based on Oprah's favorite books. "I want to make movies that will open our hearts just a little wider," Oprah says.

Star Maker

Oprah has an eye for talent. She has helped launch the careers of other TV hosts. Viewers first got to know Dr. Phil McGraw as a regular guest on *The Oprah Winfrey Show*. In 2002, Harpo Productions gave the straight-talking Texan his own talk show, *Dr. Phil*.

In 2006, Harpo helped launch the talk show career of chef Rachael Ray. She had been a regular guest on *The Oprah Winfrey Show*. Most talk shows end in failure. Rachael Ray and Dr. Phil have succeeded—with a little help from their friend Oprah.

Oprah appeared on the first episode of Rachael Ray's show.

Oprah's Web

Oprah is always looking for new ways to reach people. In 1995, she launched Oprah Online. Today, her award-winning web site, Oprah.com, attracts more than 6 million people a month. The site is very **interactive**. Oprah's viewers comment on issues and chat about books at Oprah's Book Club online. They can also get answers to questions about health and fitness.

Keeping Watch

In 2005, Oprah decided to use the Internet to target suspected child abusers. She started her own Child Predator Watch List. Within 48 hours of the web site's launch, two alleged child abusers were caught.

At Home With Oprah

Oprah's day begins before dawn. With a TV and radio show, magazines, and charities to run, she has a hectic schedule. That's why home is important to her. "Home is the place where you restore yourself," she says. At home in Chicago, her favorite room is lined with books. Oprah rarely watches television. For Oprah, television is work. To relax, she reads until she falls asleep.

A Media Empire

The Oprah Winfrey Show is the highest-rated talk show in history. Today, it reaches 46 million viewers in the United States. It's shown in 136 countries. Oprah's latest contract will keep the show on air until 2011. Her influence will be felt long after that, however. Her show's success has allowed Oprah to expand her media empire. In 2006, Oprah launched Oprah & Friends, a satellite radio channel.

Backing Obama

In 2007, Oprah got involved with politics for the first time. She decided to support Barack Obama in his bid to become president of the United States. She campaigned for him in key states. More than 18,000 people showed up for her first Obama rally in Iowa. Obama says Oprah helped him "reach some people who might not otherwise be thinking about politics."

In December 2007, Oprah joined Barack Obama at a rally in New Hampshire.

27

Her Own Network

In 2008, Oprah announced her biggest move yet. She plans to launch her own television network. By 2009, OWN: The Oprah Winfrey Network will be beaming into 70 million homes. "I always felt my show was just the beginning of what the future could hold," Oprah said.

A Lifelong Mission

Oprah is a woman on a mission. Her goal is to inspire, empower, and encourage people to live the best lives they can. In turn, she hopes they will help other people along the way. "My initial dream for myself — to create work that would touch people's lives — came true," Oprah says. "And for that, I am eternally grateful."

Time Line

1954 — Oprah Gail Winfrey is born on January 29, in Kosciusko, Mississippi.

1971 — Gets her first job reading the news at WVOL radio in Nashville, Tennessee.

1984 — Lands a job hosting *A.M. Chicago* on WLS-TV. It is renamed *The Oprah Winfrey Show* a year later.

1986 — Forms Harpo, Inc.; *The Oprah Winfrey Show* is shown nationwide for the first time.

1996 — Launches Oprah's Book Club.

1998 — Founds Oprah's Angel Network.

2000 — Launches *O, The Oprah Magazine*.

2007 — Opens the first Oprah Winfrey Leadership Academy for Girls in South Africa.

2008 — Announces she will launch her own cable network, OWN: The Oprah Winfrey Network, in 2009.

Glossary

apartheid—a former practice of separating people by race in South Africa. Apartheid required separate housing, education, employment, and transportation for white and nonwhite people.

auditioned—tried out for a role in a movie, play, or TV show

critics—in entertainment, people whose job is to give their opinions about movies, TV shows, or music

database—a large collection of information that can be searched by computer

debut—first public presentation

interactive—involving the actions of a user

Jim Crow laws—rules that required white people and black people to use separate public facilities, such as drinking fountains and telephone booths

multimedia—including several types of media, such as magazines, television, and radio

producers—people who get the money and organize the people to make a movie or TV show

racism—hatred of people because of their race or skin color

sympathetic—showing understanding of another person's feelings

To Find Out More

Books

Oprah Winfrey: The Life of a Media Superstar.
  Graphic Biographies series. Gary Jeffrey
  (Rosen Publishing Group, 2006)

Peaceful Protest: The Life of Nelson Mandela. Yona Zeldis
  McDonough (Walker Books for Young Readers, 2006)

DVDs

The Color Purple (Warner Home Video, 1997)*

The Oprah Winfrey Show 20th Anniversary Collection
  (Paramount, 2005)

Rated PG-13

Web Sites

Oprah.com
Get the scoop on all things Oprah, including Oprah's Book
Club, her TV show, and *O, The Oprah Magazine.*

www.achievement.org/autodoc/page/win0bio-1
Read an interview with Oprah and browse the photo
gallery on the Academy of Achievement site.

Index

About the Author

Jayne Keedle is a freelance writer and editor. Born in England, she lives along the Niantic River in Connecticut with her husband, Jim; stepdaughter, Alma; a chocolate Lab named Snuffles, and Phoenix the cat. Her birthday is two days before Oprah's, which makes both of them Aquarians.